DEPAOLA

❖ The Legend of ❖ the Indian Paintbrush

retold and illustrated by

Tomie dePaola

The Putnam & Grosset Group

For my dear friends,
Pat Henry and her husband, Bill,
who shared their part of Wyoming with me
and didn't make me ride a horse.
TdeP

Printed on recycled paper

A PaperStar Book,
published in 1996 by The Putnam & Grosset Group, 200 Madison Avenue,
New York, NY 10016. PaperStar is a registered trademark of
The Putnam Berkley Group, Inc. The PaperStar logo is
a trademark of The Putnam Berkley Group, Inc.
Originally published in 1988 by G. P. Putnam's Sons, New York.
Published simultaneously in Canada.
Printed in the United States of America.
Library of Congress Cataloging-in-Publication Data
dePaola, Tomie. The legend of the Indian paintbrush/retold & illustrated
by Tomie dePaola. p. cm. Summary: Little Gopher follows his destiny,
as revealed in a Dream-Vision, of becoming an artist for his people and
eventually is able to bring the colors of the sunset down to the earth.
[1. Indians of North America—Great Plains—Legends. 2. Artists—Folklore.]
I. Title. E78.G73D4 1988 398.2'08997078—dc19 [E] 87-20160
ISBN 0-698-11360-8
13 15 17 19 20 18 16 14 12

Many years ago
when the People traveled the Plains
and lived in a circle of teepees,
there was a boy who was smaller
than the rest of the children in the tribe.
No matter how hard he tried,
he couldn't keep up with the other boys
who were always riding, running, shooting their bows,
and wrestling to prove their strength.
Sometimes his mother and father worried for him.

But the boy, who was called Little Gopher,
was not without a gift of his own.
From an early age, he made toy warriors
from scraps of leather and pieces of wood
and he loved to decorate smooth stones
with the red juices from berries
he found in the hills.
The wise shaman of the tribe understood
that Little Gopher had a gift that was special.
"Do not struggle, Little Gopher.
Your path will not be the same as the others.
They will grow up to be warriors.
Your place among the People will be remembered
for a different reason."

And in a few years
when Little Gopher was older,
he went out to the hills alone
to think about becoming a man,
for this was the custom of the tribe.
And it was there that a Dream-Vision came to him.

The sky filled with clouds and out of them
came a young Indian maiden and an old grandfather.
She carried a rolled-up animal skin
and he carried a brush made of fine animal hairs
and pots of paints.

The grandfather spoke.
"My son, these are the tools
by which you shall become great among your People.
You will paint pictures of the deeds of the warriors
and the visions of the shaman,
and the People shall see them and remember them forever."

The maiden unrolled a pure white buckskin
and placed it on the ground.
"Find a buckskin as white as this," she told him.
"Keep it and one day you will paint a picture
that is as pure as the colors
in the evening sky."

And as she finished speaking, the clouds cleared
and a sunset of great beauty filled the sky.
Little Gopher looked at the white buckskin
and on it he saw colors as bright and beautiful
as those made by the setting sun.

Then the sun slowly sank behind the hills,
the sky grew dark,
and the Dream-Vision was over.
Little Gopher returned to the circle of the People.

The next day he began to make soft brushes
from the hairs of different animals
and stiff brushes from the hair of the horses' tails.
He gathered berries and flowers
and rocks of different colors
and crushed them to make his paints.

He collected the skins of animals,
which the warriors brought home from their hunts.
He stretched the skins on wooden frames
and pulled them until they were tight.

And he began to paint pictures . . .

Of great hunts . . .

Of great deeds . . .

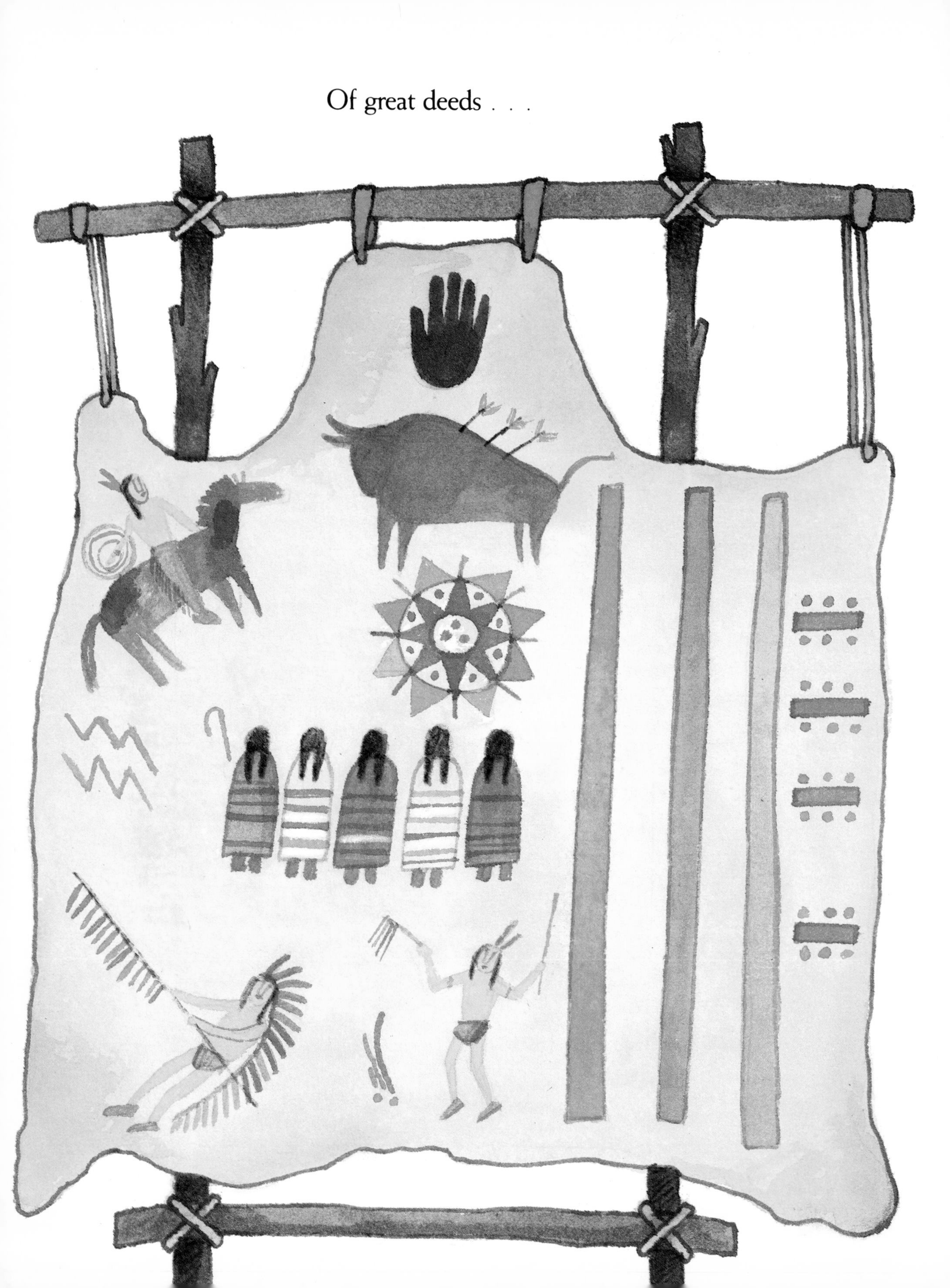

Of great Dream-Visions . . .
So that the People would always remember.

But even as he painted,
Little Gopher sometimes longed
to put aside his brushes
and ride out with the warriors.
But always he remembered his Dream-Vision
and he did not go with them.

Many months ago,
he had found his pure white buckskin,
but it remained empty
because he could not find the colors of the sunset.
He used the brightest flowers,
the reddest berries,
and the deepest purples from the rocks,
and still his paintings never satisfied him.
They looked dull and dark.

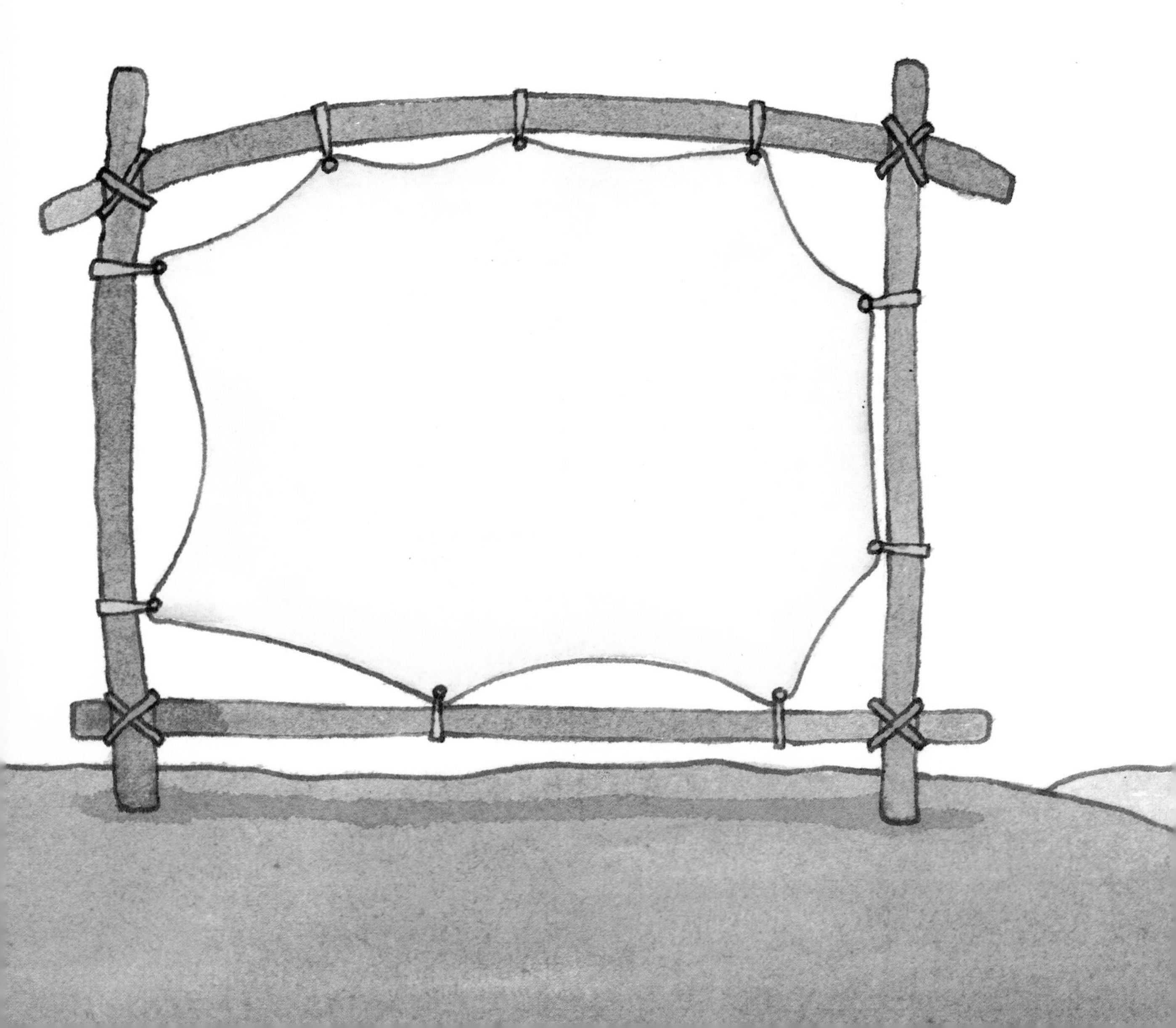

He began to go to the top of a hill each evening
and look at the colors that filled the sky
to try and understand how to make them.
He longed to share the beauty of his Dream-Vision
with the People.

But he never gave up trying,
and every morning when he awoke
he took out his brushes and his pots of paints
and created the stories of the People
with the tools he had.

One night as he lay awake,
he heard a voice calling to him.
"Because you have been faithful to the People
and true to your gift,
you shall find the colors you are seeking.

Tomorrow take the white buckskin
and go to the place
where you watch the sun in the evening.
There on the ground you will find what you need."

The next evening as the sun began to go down,
Little Gopher put aside his brushes
and went to the top of the hill
as the colors of the sunset spread across the sky.

And there, on the ground all around him,
were brushes filled with paint,
each one a color of the sunset.
Little Gopher began to paint quickly and surely,
using one brush, then another.

And as the colors in the sky began to fade,
Little Gopher gazed at the white buckskin
and he was happy.
He had found the colors of the sunset.
He carried his painting down
to the circle of the People,
leaving the brushes on the hillside.

And the next day, when the People awoke,
the hill was ablaze with color,
for the brushes had taken root in the earth
and multiplied into plants
of brilliant reds, oranges and yellows.

And every spring from that time,
the hills and meadows burst into bloom.

And every spring,
the People danced and sang the praises
of Little Gopher who had painted for the People.

And the People no longer called him Little Gopher,
but He-Who-Brought-the-Sunset-to-the-Earth.

Author's Note

The lovely red, orange, yellow (and even pink) Indian Paintbrush blooms in profusion throughout Wyoming, Texas, and the high plains, and has many stories connected with its origin. The story of the Native American artist and his desire to paint the sunset was particularly meaningful to me as an artist. (There are many times when I wish I could go out on a hill and find brushes filled with exactly the colors I need. Who knows . . . someday maybe . . .)

The idea for doing a book on this spectacular wildflower came from my good friend Pat Henry after she had seen my book *The Legend of the Bluebonnet,* which is the story of the Texas state flower. Pat is from Wyoming where the Indian Paintbrush is the state flower.

Coincidentally, Carolyn Sullivan from Austin, Texas, had recently sent me a copy of *Texas Wildflowers, Stories and Legends,* a collection of articles by Ruth D. Isely which originally appeared in the *Austin American-Statesman.* Carolyn is a teacher in the Austin area, and in 1965 this collection was made available to teachers there for use with a unit on Texas trees and wildflowers. She too had read the bluebonnet book and knew of my deep interest in folktale and legend.

The Indian Paintbrush is a familiar flower to Texans and in the book I came across a brief and interesting account of how the wildflower got its name. I contacted Mrs. Isely and she graciously gave me permission to use her article as the main source for my retelling of the legend of the Indian Paintbrush.

So, I would like to thank Pat Henry for suggesting the book, Carolyn Sullivan for sending me the collection of legends and Ruth Isely for giving me inspiration from her collection. I would also like to thank and acknowledge Lady Bird Johnson, the former First Lady, whose untiring efforts have not only made her home state of Texas a symphony of color with its wildflowers, but have encouraged other states throughout the country in the preserving and growing of native wildflowers to beautify the countryside.

TdeP N.H.

Property of
BRIDGEPORT PUBLIC LIBRARY
Old Mill Green Library